UNVEILING

CORDOBA

Your Travel Guide to Andalusia's Mesmeric Oasis

presented by

Discover your journey!

Presented by Tailored Travel Guides
a WEST AGORA INT S.R.L. Brand
www.tailoredtravelguides.com

Edited by WEST AGORA INT S.R.L.
WEST AGORA INT S.R.L. All Rights Reserved
Copyright © WEST AGORA INT S.R.L., 2023

WIKI

Córdoba, a mesmerizing city situated in the southern heartland of Spain, stands as a living testament to the diverse cultures that have shaped its history. Located in the sun-drenched region of Andalusia, Córdoba's past is a blend of Roman, Islamic, and Christian influences, each leaving an indelible mark on its landscape.

Founded by the Romans, Córdoba's strategic location along the Guadalquivir River made it a significant hub of trade and politics. However, its true golden age dawned during Islamic rule, when it became the capital of the Caliphate of Córdoba. During this period, the city emerged as a center of education, culture, and architectural marvels, rivaling the grandeur of Constantinople and Baghdad.

The Mezquita, an architectural masterpiece, stands as a testament to this era. Originally a mosque, it was later converted into a cathedral, symbolizing the city's religious evolution. Its intricate arches and columns are a visual representation of Córdoba's blended heritage.

Yet, Córdoba's legacy isn't solely anchored in its Islamic past. The Roman Bridge, Alcázar, and the remnants of Roman temples whisper tales of an era where gladiators and senators walked its streets. The Jewish Quarter, with its narrow alleys and Sephardic history, adds another layer to the city's rich tapestry, with figures like Maimonides shaping its intellectual legacy.

Today, Córdoba is celebrated for its festivals, notably the Feria de los Patios, where courtyards bloom in a riot of colors. Its gastronomy, a blend of Moorish and Spanish flavors, tantalizes the palate, making it a culinary destination.

However, like any historical city, Córdoba faces challenges. Balancing modernity with its rich heritage, addressing the needs of its growing population while preserving its historical sites, and navigating the complexities of regional identity in a globalized world are issues at its forefront.

Notable figures, including Seneca the Younger, a Roman philosopher, and Averroes, an Islamic polymath, hail from Córdoba. Yet, its history is tinged with controversies, especially during the Reconquista and the subsequent Spanish Inquisition, periods that tested its harmonious multicultural legacy.

In essence, Córdoba is more than just a city; it's a chronicle of civilizations, a blend of cultures, and a testament to the enduring spirit of humanity's quest for knowledge, art, and coexistence. It beckons travelers to journey through time, offering a glimpse into the tapestry of cultures that is quintessentially Spain.

CONTENTS

1   GREETINGS AND RECOMMENDATIONS FROM LOCALS

PRACTICAL INFORMATION   2

6   TOP ATTRACTIONS IN CORDOBA

HIDDEN GEMS AND LESSER-KNOWN SIGHTS IN CORDOBA   10

13   PARKS AND GARDENS IN CORDOBA

CORDOBA'S CULINARY SCENE   15

17   SHOPPING IN CORDOBA

FAMILY-FRIENDLY ACTIVITIES IN CORDOBA   19

21   CORDOBA BY NIGHT

ART AND CULTURE IN CORDOBA   27

30   HISTORICAL AND ARCHITECTURAL LANDMARKS IN CORDOBA

DAY TRIPS FROM CORDOBA   33

35   END NOTE

CORDOBA

ANDALUSIA'S MESMERIC OASIS

Cordoba, the Timeless Jewel of Andalusia
Nestled in the heart of southern Spain, Cordoba is a mesmerizing blend of ancient civilizations and contemporary vibrancy. This enchanting city, once the capital of Islamic Spain, showcases an intricate tapestry of Moorish artistry, Christian grandeur, and Jewish heritage. The majestic Mezquita, with its forest of columns and intricate arches, stands in harmony with the lively patios adorned with colorful flowers, reflecting Cordoba's rich mosaic of cultures.

A Melody of Historical Grandeur and Andalusian Flair
Cordoba's narrow alleyways echo with the soulful strums of the Spanish guitar, merging with the poetic verses of Andalusian ballads. As a culinary delight of Spain, the city's cuisine offers a delectable fusion of Mediterranean flavors and Moorish influences, with every dish narrating a story of its diverse heritage. The scent of orange blossoms mingles with the rich aroma of traditional stews, capturing the essence of Cordoba's gastronomic legacy. Under the starlit sky, the Alcazar gardens come alive with tales of sultans, caliphs, and flamenco passion.

Your Portal to the Mystique of Andalusian Splendor
This guide is your key to unlocking Cordoba's myriad wonders. From the winding streets of the Jewish Quarter to the awe-inspiring palaces of the Alcazar, from the Roman Bridge that spans the Guadalquivir River to the vibrant festivals that celebrate the city's multifaceted heritage, we beckon you to delve into these pages and discover the heart of Cordoba. Whether you're drawn to its architectural marvels, culinary delights, or the seamless fusion of cultures, Cordoba offers an unforgettable odyssey for every traveler.

GREETINGS AND INSIGHTS FROM LOCALS

¡Bienvenido, dear traveler! Welcome to Córdoba, the enchanting jewel of Andalusia, where the echoes of a storied past harmonize with the lively rhythms of the present. As a Cordobés, I've wandered our city's cobbled lanes and blossoming patios, and I'm delighted to unveil the intimate corners and vibrant traditions that only a true local would embrace.

Begin your Córdoban journey by immersing in our heartfelt customs. A gentle "buenas" and a genuine smile can kindle lifelong bonds as you meander through the city's Moorish archways, ornate courtyards, and fragrant orange groves.

Perhaps you'll be seduced by the allure of the Judería, Córdoba's ancient Jewish Quarter. Here, centuries-old streets whisper tales of sages and scholars, and every stone recounts stories of a harmonious coexistence, juxtaposing the city's vibrant modern ethos.

For a touch of the divine, direct your steps to the Mezquita-Catedral. This architectural marvel, an emblem of Córdoba's rich tapestry of cultures, marries Islamic artistry and Christian grandeur in a dance of arches and altars, symbolizing a historic crossroad of faiths.

When your appetite stirs, venture to the bustling Mercado Victoria. Savor local delicacies, from salmorejo to flamenquín. But the pièce de résistance? Rabo de toro. Remember, we Cordobeses cherish our oxtail stew, a dish steeped in tradition and infused with Andalusian zest.

As twilight drapes its silken veil, contemplate a leisurely promenade beside the Guadalquivir River. The gentle ripple of waters, paired with melodies from nearby tabernas, composes a captivating serenade.

At the city's epicenter, the Alcázar de los Reyes Cristianos beckons. With its majestic gardens and reflective ponds, this fortress stands as a testament to Córdoba's regal legacy. Ascend its towers for panoramic vistas that render every heartbeat in awe.

As you traverse Córdoba, let its mesmerizing blend of histories and horizons enrapture your senses. We, the locals, stand with open arms, ready to share the magic of our timeless city with you. ¡Hasta pronto, dear traveler, and may your journey through Córdoba be etched with indelible memories!

PRACTICAL INFORMATION

Currency
Spain uses the Euro (€) as its currency. In Cordoba, credit cards are commonly accepted in most establishments, including restaurants and larger shops. However, when visiting smaller boutiques, local eateries, or market stalls, it's a good idea to have some cash on hand.

Transportation
Córdoba is well-connected by train, bus, and road. The city's main train station, Córdoba Central, offers high-speed connections to major Spanish cities. Local buses are a convenient way to get around the city, and taxis are readily available.

Driving in Cordoba
While the city center is pedestrian-friendly, driving can be challenging due to narrow streets and limited parking. It's advisable to park outside the historic center and explore on foot.

Climate
Córdoba experiences a Mediterranean climate with hot summers and mild winters. The city is known for its scorching temperatures in July and August, so it's essential to stay hydrated and avoid outdoor activities during peak hours.

Language
Spanish is the official language. However, English is commonly understood in tourist areas.

Power sockets and adapters
Spain uses Type F sockets with a standard voltage of 230V and a frequency of 50Hz. Travelers from countries with different socket types may need an adapter.

Shopping
Córdoba offers a range of shopping experiences, from traditional souvenirs to high-end boutiques. Don't miss the local craft markets showcasing leather goods, ceramics, and jewelry.

Tipping
Tipping is not mandatory in Spain, but it's customary to leave a small amount (5-10%) for good service in restaurants and cafes.

PRACTICAL INFORMATION

USEFUL LINKS AND PHONE NUMBERS

Emergency Services
All Emergencies: 112
Police: 092
Fire Brigade: 080
Medical Emergencies: 061

Transportation
Córdoba Central Train Station: +34 902 432 343, www.renfe.com/es/en
Córdoba Bus Station: +34 957 404 444, www.estacionautobusescordoba.es
Local Buses (AUCORSA): +34 957 764 444, www.aucorsa.es

Tourist Information
Córdoba Tourism Office: +34 957 491 678, www.turismodecordoba.org
Tourist Map www.ontheworldmap.com/spain/city/cordoba/cordoba-street-map.jpg

Hospitals
Hospital Universitario Reina Sofía: +34 957 010 000, http://www.sspa.juntadeandalucia.es/servicioandaluzdesalud/hrs3/index.php?id=portada
Hospital San Juan de Dios: +34 957 420 100, https://hsjdcordoba.sjd.es/

Local Government
City of Córdoba: +34 957 499 900, www.cordoba.es

Maps
Cordoba maps: www.ontheworldmap.com/spain/city/cordoba/
Cordoba City Center: www.ontheworldmap.com/spain/city/cordoba/cordoba-street-map.jpg
Cordoba Tourist Map: www.ontheworldmap.com/spain/city/cordoba/cordoba-tourist-map.jpg

PRACTICAL INFORMATION
CORDOBA CITY CENTER MAP

Free high resolution download at: www.ontheworldmap.com/spain/city/cordoba/cordoba-street-map.jpg

PRACTICAL INFORMATION
CORDOBA TOURIST MAP

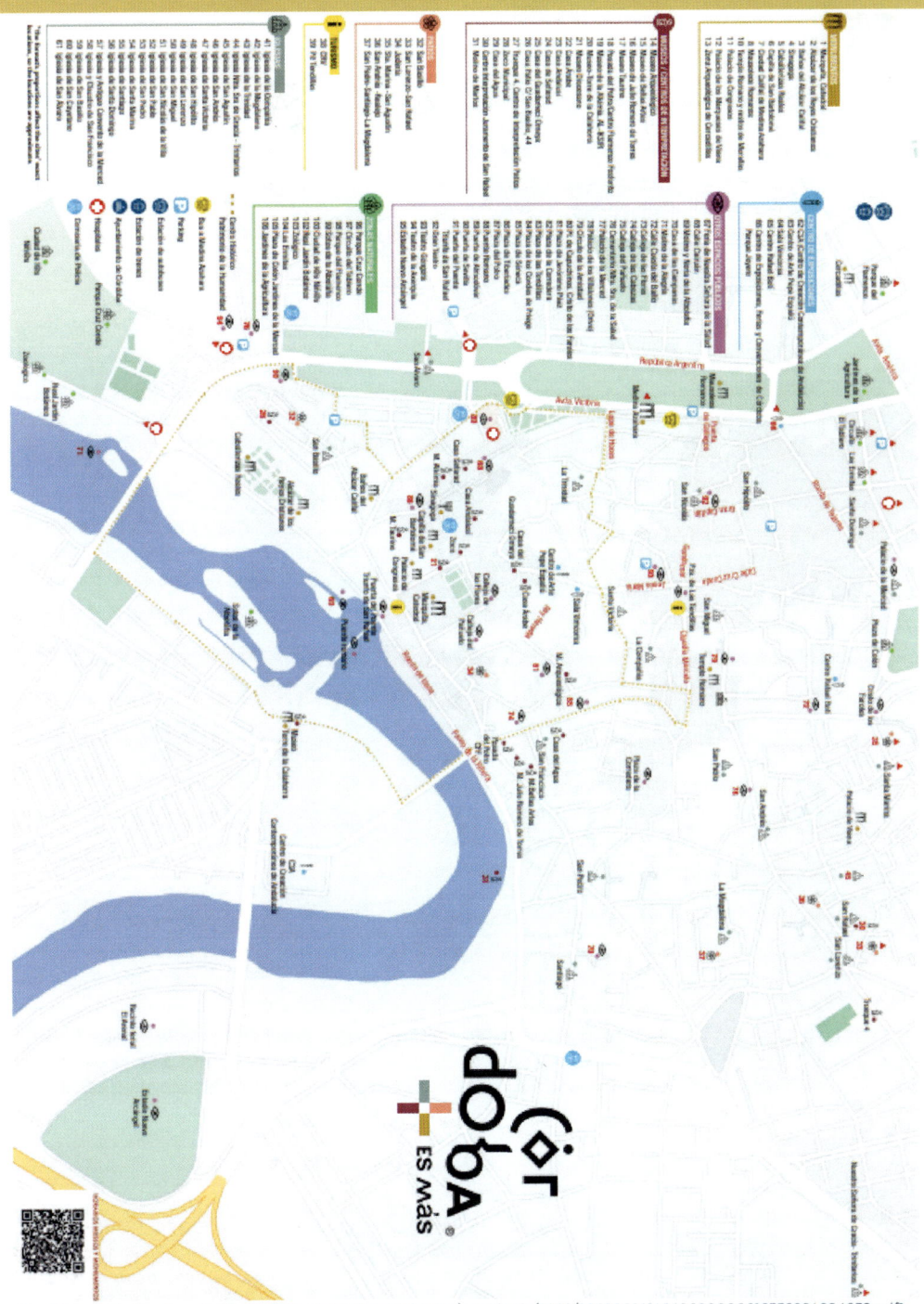

TOP ATTRACTIONS IN CORDOBA

MOSQUE-CATHEDRAL OF CÓRDOBA

The Mezquita-Catedral is an architectural marvel that showcases the rich history of Córdoba. Originally a mosque, it was converted into a cathedral in the 13th century. Its stunning arches, intricate mosaics, and the blend of Moorish and Christian architecture make it a must-visit. This UNESCO World Heritage site stands as a testament to the city's diverse cultural influences, with its prayer niches, chapels, and the iconic bell tower offering panoramic views of Córdoba.

Location: C. Cardenal Herrero, 1, 14003 Córdoba, Spain

Website: www.mezquita-catedraldecordoba.es/en/

Tip: Arrive early to avoid the crowds. Consider taking a guided tour to fully appreciate its history, architectural nuances, and the stories behind its transformation.

ALCÁZAR DE LOS REYES CRISTIANOS

This fortress-palace, once home to Catholic Monarchs Ferdinand and Isabella, boasts beautiful gardens, fountains, and impressive towers offering panoramic views of the city. Its rich history is palpable, from its role in the Reconquista to being the setting for Christopher Columbus's audience with the monarchs. The architecture seamlessly blends Roman and Moorish styles, with intricate tilework and lush courtyards that transport visitors to a bygone era. The walls echo tales of royal gatherings, strategic meetings, and cultural exchanges, making it a living testament to Spain's diverse heritage. The Alcázar also played a significant role during the Inquisition, adding another layer to its multifaceted history.

Location: C. Caballerizas Reales, s/n, 14004 Córdoba, Spain

Website: www.alcazardelosreyescristianos.cordoba.es/?id=3

Tip: Don't miss the mosaic-filled Roman baths in the basement. Allocate time to wander the gardens, reflect by the tranquil ponds, and immerse yourself in the stories of the past. Climbing the towers provides a unique perspective on the city's layout and its surrounding.

TOP ATTRACTIONS IN CORDOBA

ROMAN BRIDGE

Spanning the Guadalquivir River, this ancient bridge offers a scenic walk with views of the Mezquita and the old town. It has been restored several times since its initial construction during the Roman era. The bridge, with its 16 arches and historic significance, stands as a testament to the engineering prowess of the Romans and has played a pivotal role in Córdoba's history, connecting different parts of the city for centuries.
Location: Av. del Alcázar, s/n, 14009 Córdoba, Spain
Website: www.turismodecordoba.org/puente-romano
Tip: Visit during sunset for a breathtaking view. The golden hues reflecting off the stone provide a magical backdrop, enhancing the bridge's timeless beauty.

MEDINA AZAHARA

An ancient Moorish city located just outside Córdoba, Medina Azahara is a testament to the opulence of the Caliphate era. As a UNESCO World Heritage site, it showcases the grandeur of Islamic art and architecture, with its intricate carvings, expansive courtyards, and remnants of once-majestic palaces. The ruins paint a vivid picture of the city's past splendor and cultural significance.
Location: Ctra. Palma del Río, km 5.5, 14005 Córdoba, Spain
Website: www.turismodecordoba.org/medina-azahara-1
Tip: Take a guided tour to understand the historical significance of the ruins and immerse yourself in the stories of its golden age.

TOP ATTRACTIONS IN CORDOBA

PALACIO DE VIANA

Known as the 'Museum of Patios', Palacio de Viana stands as a captivating blend of history and beauty in the heart of Córdoba. A testament to Andalusian architecture and garden design, this palace boasts 12 distinct courtyards, each radiating its unique style, charm, and lush greenery. Wander through rooms adorned with valuable artworks, antiques, intricate tapestries, and historical artifacts, each telling tales of the city's rich past and the palace's aristocratic elegance.

Location: Pl. de Don Gome, 2, 14001 Córdoba, Spain
Website: www.palaciodeviana.com
Tip: Beyond its architectural splendor, the palace frequently hosts cultural events. It's recommended to check their calendar for special exhibitions, workshops, or performances during your visit.

JEWISH QUARTER (JUDERÍA)

The Judería, Córdoba's historic Jewish Quarter, is a mesmerizing maze of narrow, winding streets that transport visitors back in time. Lined with white-washed houses adorned with vibrant flowers and intricate ironwork, this area echoes tales of a bygone era. As you stroll, you'll encounter significant landmarks, ancient synagogues, and hidden courtyards, each bearing witness to Córdoba's rich multicultural tapestry. The area stands as a testament to the harmonious coexistence of Muslim, Christian, and Jewish cultures, making it a vital part of the city's heritage.

Location: C. Judíos, 20, 14004 Córdoba, Spain
Website: www.turismodecordoba.org/the-jewish-quarter
Tip: While exploring, make a point to visit the Casa de Sefarad. This museum offers a profound insight into the history, traditions, and contributions of the Jewish community in Córdoba.

TOP ATTRACTIONS IN CORDOBA

SINAGOGA DE CÓRDOBA

A testament to Córdoba's rich Jewish heritage, the Sinagoga de Córdoba stands as one of the few preserved synagogues from the medieval period in Spain. Its exquisite Mudejar-style architecture, complemented by intricate stucco work and profound Hebrew inscriptions, offers a glimpse into the spiritual and artistic life of the Jewish community of the time. This sacred space resonates with history and cultural significance.
Location: Calle Judíos, 20, 14004 Córdoba
Website:
www.juntadeandalucia.es/cultura/enclaves/enclave-monumental-sinagoga-de-cordoba
Tip: Given its intimate size, consider visiting during off-peak times to fully appreciate its beauty and serenity.

CALLEJA DE LAS FLORES

A picturesque alley filled with potted flowers, it's one of the most photographed spots in Córdoba. The end of the alley offers a unique view of the Mezquita's tower.
Location: Calleja de las Flores, 14003 Córdoba
Website:
www.andalucia.org/en/cordoba-cultural-tourism-calleja-de-las-flores
Tip: Visit in May during the Festival of Patios when the alley is in full bloom.

PUERTA DEL PUENTE

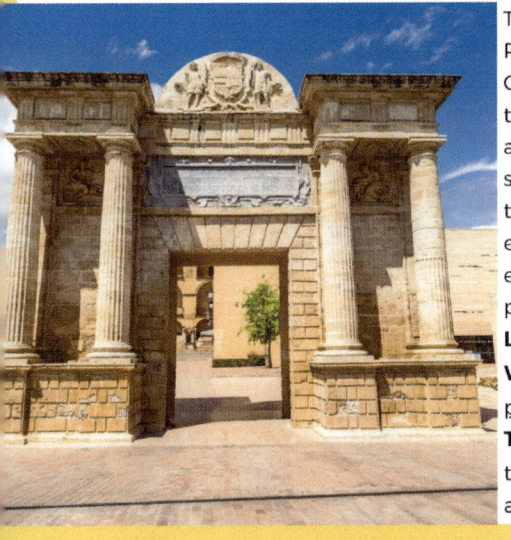

The majestic Puerta del Puente, a splendid Renaissance gate, stands tall as a testament to Córdoba's illustrious past. Historically, it marked the main entrance to the city, welcoming travelers and traders from distant lands. Flanked by robust stone walls and adorned with intricate carvings, this architectural marvel beautifully captures the essence of Córdoba's fusion of cultures and epochs. Its strategic location near the river offers a panoramic view of the city's skyline.
Location: Pl. del Triunfo, s/n, 14003 Córdoba, Spain
Website: www.turismodecordoba.org/puerta-del-puente
Tip: Begin your exploration of Córdoba here, and then meander along the iconic Roman Bridge for a journey through time.

HIDDEN GEMS AND LESSER-KNOWN SIGHTS IN CORDOBA

TORRE DE LA CALAHORRA

An emblematic sentinel, the Calahorra Tower proudly guards the southern end of Córdoba's Roman Bridge. Erected in the late 12th century by the Almohads, its robust structure was further fortified by the Christians. Beyond its historical facade, the tower is home to a museum that vividly narrates Córdoba's rich tapestry of cultures. It emphasizes the harmonious coexistence of Judaism, Christianity, and Islam, shedding light on their intertwined histories and shared heritage.
Location: Puente Romano, s/n, 14009 Córdoba, Spain
Tip: Ascend the tower for a mesmerizing view of the city's landscape, particularly enchanting as the sun dips below the horizon.
Website: www.torrecalahorra.es

CASA ANDALUSÍ

A hidden gem in the heart of the Jewish Quarter, Casa Andalusí offers a glimpse into the life of a 12th-century Andalusian home. It features a beautiful patio, ancient Roman mosaics, and a well-preserved Jewish cellar.
Location: C. Judíos, 12, 14004 Córdoba, Spain
Tip: Don't miss the ancient Roman mosaic on the ground floor.
Website: http://lacasaandalusi.com/casaandalusi/

BATHS OF THE CALIPHATE

Nestled close to the Alcázar, the Baths of the Caliphate transport visitors to Córdoba's illustrious Moorish era. These ancient Arab baths, with their intricately designed arches and serene ambiance, served not just as a place for purification but also as hubs of social interaction during the Caliphate period. The delicate play of light through the star-shaped openings in the ceiling adds to the ethereal experience, evoking a sense of timelessness and connection to the city's opulent past.
Location: Plaza Campo Santo de los Mártires s/n. 14004. Córdoba
Tip: To fully immerse in its tranquility, consider visiting early in the morning, sidestepping the usual bustle.
Website: www.turismodecordoba.org/caliphal-baths

HIDDEN GEMS AND LESSER-KNOWN SIGHTS IN CORDOBA

TEMPLO ROMANO

Tucked away in the heart of Córdoba lies the Templo Romano, a majestic testament to the city's Roman legacy. Dating back to the 1st century AD, this once-magnificent temple, with its towering columns and classical architecture, stood as a symbol of Roman power and influence. Today, while only a few columns and the foundation remain, they paint a vivid picture of the temple's past grandeur and the rich tapestry of cultures that have shaped Córdoba.
Location: C. Capitulares, 1, 14002 Córdoba, Spain
Tip: For a truly enchanting experience, visit after dusk when the ruins are bathed in a soft, golden glow.
Website: www.turismodecordoba.org/templo-romano-de-cordoba

CASA DE LAS CABEZAS

Nestled in the heart of Córdoba, the Casa de las Cabezas stands as a testament to the city's vibrant past. Named for the seven heads adorning its façade, this historic house beautifully captures traditional Andalusian architecture. Its series of enchanting patios, adorned with lush plants and intricate tiles, transport visitors to a bygone era. Delve into its corridors to uncover tales of nobility, love, and intrigue that have shaped its rich history.
Location: C. Cabezas, 18, 14003 Córdoba, Spain
Tip: The house frequently serves as a backdrop for cultural events and exhibitions, offering a unique blend of history and art.
Website: www.historicopenhouse.com/en/

CASA RAMÓN GARCÍA ROMERO

Nestled in the heart of Córdoba, Casa Ramón García Romero is a haven for traditional leather embossing. This vibrant workshop offers a glimpse into the meticulous process. Visitors can watch skilled artisans breathe life into leather. Beyond just observing, guests have the opportunity to purchase these handcrafted items,.
Location: Pl. Agrupación de Cofradías, 2, 14003 Córdoba, Spain
Tip: The handcrafted leather goods make for unique souvenirs.
Website: www.guadameciomeya.com/en/

CASA DEL BAILÍO

Nestled in the heart of Córdoba, Casa del Bailío stands as an architectural marvel. Beyond its stunning Mudejar-style coffered ceiling, the house beautifully encapsulates the intricate blend of Christian and Moorish influences. Its walls whisper tales of bygone eras, making it a living testament to the city's rich history and the confluence of diverse cultures.
Location: C. Cta. del Bailío, 3, 14001 Córdoba, Spain
Tip: While exploring, keep an eye out for the temporary art exhibitions that often grace its halls, adding to its cultural allure.
Website: www.bibliotecavivadeal-andalus.es

PALACIO DE ORIVE

Located in the heart of Córdoba, the Palacio de Orive, also known as the Palacio de los Villalones, is a Renaissance-style mansion built in the 16th century. It boasts a beautiful patio, ornate balconies, and intricate stonework. The palace is now used as a cultural space, hosting various exhibitions, concerts, and events throughout the year. Its serene gardens are a perfect spot for relaxation, offering a peaceful escape from the bustling city.
Location: Pl. de Orive, 2, 14002 Córdoba, Spain
Tip: Check the local event listings to catch an art exhibition or musical performance during your visit.
Website: www.turismodecordoba.org/palacio-de-orive
(You might need to search for specific events or exhibitions related to Palacio de Orive on the official tourism website.)

PARKS AND GARDENS IN CORDOBA

JARDINES DEL ALCÁZAR

Located within the Alcázar de los Reyes Cristianos, these gardens are a serene blend of fountains, ponds, and beautifully manicured plants. The gardens reflect the Moorish influence with their geometric designs and water features.
Location: Plaza Campo Santo de los Mártires, Córdoba.
Tip: The gardens are especially beautiful during spring when the flowers are in full bloom.
Website: www.turismodecordoba.org/alcazar-de-los-reyes-cristianos

JARDINES DE LA AGRICULTURA

Nestled in the heart of Córdoba, Jardines de la Agricultura is a lush oasis boasting a diverse collection of trees, vibrant flowerbeds, and artistic sculptures. This expansive park offers serene pathways, shaded benches, and charming fountains, making it an ideal retreat for relaxation and nature appreciation. Whether you're looking for a peaceful walk, a family picnic, or simply a moment of tranquility, this garden is a must-visit.
Location: Av. de los Mozárabes, 3, 14011 Córdoba, Spain
Tip: Don't miss the iconic statue of the woman with the water jug, a favorite among visitors for capturing memories.
Website: www.turismodecordoba.org/jardines-de-la-agricultura

JARDINES JUAN CARLOS I

A tribute to King Juan Carlos I, this contemporary park seamlessly blends nature and urban design. With its meticulously landscaped gardens, vibrant flower beds, and meandering pathways, it offers a refreshing escape in the city. Children delight in the well-equipped playgrounds, while the soothing sounds of fountains create a serene ambiance. From seasonal events to local fairs, there's always something happening, making it a dynamic hub for both locals and tourists.
Location: C. Antonio Maura, 29, 14004 Córdoba, Spain
Tip: If visiting with kids, the playgrounds are a must-try. Also, keep an eye out for cultural events and weekend fairs.
Website: www.turismodecordoba.org/jardines-de-juan-carlos-i

PARKS AND GARDENS IN CORDOBA

PARQUE DE MIRAFLORES

Perched above the Guadalquivir River, Parque de Miraflores is a tranquil oasis offering breathtaking city panoramas. With its meticulously curated gardens, meandering pathways, and ample seating spots, it's an ideal place for relaxation and reflection. The park's elevated position provides a unique vantage point, making it a favorite among photographers and nature lovers.
Location: Calle Miraflores, Córdoba.
Tip: For a magical experience, time your visit around sunset and watch the city glow in golden hues.
Website: https://es.wikipedia.org/wiki/Parque_de_Miraflores_(C%C3%B3rdoba)

PARQUE DE LA ASOMADILLA

Nestled in the heart of Córdoba, Jardines de la Victoria offers a harmonious fusion of historical landmarks and verdant beauty. With its diverse flora, mesmerizing fountains, and significant monuments, it's a serene escape from urban hustle. The iconic "Kiosk of the Victoria" within the gardens frequently hosts vibrant events, making it a cultural hub for locals and tourists alike.
Location: Paseo de la Victoria, Córdoba.
Tip: Don't miss the lively performances at the historic kiosk, especially during evenings.
Website: www.turismodecordoba.org/gardens-of-la-victoria-cordoba

PARQUE DE LA ASOMADILLA

One of the largest green spaces in Córdoba, Parque de la Asomadilla offers expansive meadows, children's play areas, and a serene pond. Its elevated position provides panoramic views of the city, making it a popular spot for both relaxation and recreation.
Location: Escultor Pablo Gargallo, s/n, 14006 Córdoba, Spain
Tip: The park's observation deck is a must-visit for breathtaking views, especially during sunset.
Website:
www.turismodecordoba.org/parque-de-la-asomadilla

CORDOBA'S CULINARY SCENE

RESTAURANTE EL CHURRASCO

A renowned establishment in Córdoba, El Churrasco offers a delightful blend of traditional Andalusian flavors with a modern twist. Their grilled meats, especially the namesake "churrasco," are a must-try.
Location: Calle Romero, 16, Córdoba.
Tip: Pair your meal with a local wine for an authentic Cordoban dining experience.
Website: www.elchurrasco.com

CASA PEPE DE LA JUDERÍA

Nestled in the historic Jewish quarter, Casa Pepe is known for its traditional Cordoban dishes and a charming ambiance. The patio seating offers a picturesque view of the Mezquita.
Location: Calle Romero, 1, Córdoba.
Tip: Try the "flamenquín," a local delicacy,.
Website: www.restaurantecasapepedelajuderia.co

TABERNA LA MONTILLANA

A rustic tavern that captures the essence of Córdoba's culinary heritage. Their tapas selection is extensive and flavorful.
Location: Calle San Álvaro, 5, Córdoba.
Tip: The "salmorejo" here is a crowd favorite. Don't miss it!
Website: www.tabernalamontillana.com

BODEGAS CAMPOS

A historic bodega turned restaurant, Campos offers a unique dining experience. The traditional Cordoban dishes are complemented by their vast selection of wines.
Location: Calle Los Lineros, 32, Córdoba.
Tip: Book a wine tasting session to explore the rich flavors of the region.
Website: www.bodegascampos.com

CORDOBA'S CULINARY SCENE

SALMOREJO CORDOBÉS

A cold tomato soup, Salmorejo is thickened with bread and seasoned with garlic and vinegar. Topped with hard-boiled eggs and jamón serrano, it's a refreshing dish perfect for warm days.

Tip: Best enjoyed with a slice of fresh bread.

PASTEL CORDOBÉS

A delightful pastry filled with sweet pumpkin jam and sprinkled with sugar on top. It's a traditional dessert that captures the essence of Córdoba's sweet treats.

Tip: Pair it with a cup of local coffee for a perfect end to your meal.

FINO

A dry, pale white sherry wine, Fino is produced in the Montilla-Moriles region near Córdoba. It's best served chilled and is a perfect accompaniment to tapas.

Tip: Fino is also used in cooking, especially in traditional Cordoban dishes.

FLAMENQUÍN

A popular Andalusian dish, Flamenquín consists of ham-wrapped meat (usually pork), coated in breadcrumbs and deep-fried. It's often served with fries or a salad.

Tip: Squeeze a bit of lemon on top for an added zest.

SHOPPING IN CORDOBA

MERCADO VICTORIA

Mercado Victoria is Córdoba's first gastronomic market. Housed in a 19th-century wrought iron structure, it offers a blend of traditional and modern stalls. From fresh produce to gourmet delicacies, there's something for every palate.
Location: Paseo de la Victoria, s/n, Córdoba.
Tip: Don't miss the local cheese and olive oil stalls. They offer some of the region's finest products.
Website: www.mercadovictoria.com

CALLEJA DE LAS FLORES SHOPS

One of the most picturesque streets in Córdoba, Calleja de las Flores is not just about the vibrant flowers and charming ambiance. The narrow alley is lined with quaint shops selling traditional crafts, souvenirs, and local artifacts.
Location: Calleja de las Flores, Córdoba.
Tip: Look out for handmade ceramics and leather goods. They make for perfect souvenirs to take back home.

CALLE CRUZ CONDE

As one of the main shopping streets in Córdoba, Calle Cruz Conde is bustling with activity. From high-end boutiques to local brands, the street offers a diverse shopping experience.
Location: Calle Cruz Conde, Córdoba.
Tip: The street is pedestrianized, making it a pleasant experience to stroll and shop at leisure. Don't forget to take a break at one of the many cafes lining the street.
Website: www.turismodecordoba.org/calle-cruz-conde2

SHOPPING IN CORDOBA

PLAZA DE LAS TENDILLAS

Plaza de las Tendillas is the heart of Córdoba's shopping district. This spacious square is surrounded by a variety of shops, from well-known international brands to local boutiques.
Location: Plaza de las Tendillas, Córdoba.
Tip: The plaza is a great place to relax after a shopping spree. Enjoy the musical fountain show in the evenings, especially during the summer months.
Website: www.turismodecordoba.org/plaza-de-las-tendillas2

CASA ÁRABE

Casa Árabe is not just a cultural center but also a shopping haven for those interested in Middle Eastern and Andalusian crafts. The shop within offers a curated selection of books, handicrafts, and unique souvenirs that reflect the Arab influence on Córdoba.
Location: Calle Samuel de los Santos Gener, 9, Córdoba.
Tip: After shopping, visit the exhibitions and events that Casa Árabe regularly hosts to get a deeper understanding of Arab-Andalusian culture.
Website: www.casaarabe.es

CASA DEL BAILÍO

Located in a historic building, Casa del Bailío is a treasure trove for art and antique lovers. The shop specializes in antiques, paintings, and decorative items, each telling a story of Córdoba's rich past.
Location: Calle del Bailío, Córdoba.
Tip: Even if you're not looking to buy, the shop is worth a visit for its beautifully preserved architecture and the array of historical items on display.
Website: www.turismodecordoba.org/cuesta-del-bailio

FAMILY-FRIENDLY ACTIVITIES IN CORDOBA

CÓRDOBA ZOO

Córdoba Zoo offers a delightful experience for families, with a diverse range of animals from around the world. The zoo places a strong emphasis on conservation and education, making it not only entertaining but also informative. From African elephants to exotic birds, there's plenty to see and learn.

Location: Av. Linneo, s/n, 14071 Córdoba, Spain

Tip: Don't miss the interactive sessions where zookeepers share fascinating facts about the animals. It's both educational and fun for kids.

Zoo Map: https://zoo.cordoba.es/mapa/
Website: https://zoo.cordoba.es/

PARQUE PERIURBANO LOS VILLARES

A haven for nature lovers, Parque Periurbano Los Villares is a sprawling green space perfect for family outings. With well-marked trails, picnic areas, and playgrounds, it's an ideal spot for hiking, bird-watching, or simply relaxing amidst nature.

Location: Carretera Vecinal Córdoba - Obejo, Km 7.5, 14012 Córdoba, Spain

Tip: The park is vast, so consider packing a picnic. There are designated areas where families can enjoy a meal amidst the scenic beauty.

Website: www.turismodecordoba.org/los-villares-periurban-country-park

CÓRDOBA BOTANICAL GARDEN

Description: The Córdoba Botanical Garden is a serene oasis that showcases a diverse range of plant species. With themed sections, including a tropical greenhouse and a Mediterranean garden, families can learn about various ecosystems and the importance of conservation.

Location: Av. de Linneo, s/n, Córdoba.

Tip: The garden often has educational programs tailored for children, teaching them about botany in a fun and engaging manner.

Website:
www.jardinbotanicodecordoba.com

FAMILY-FRIENDLY ACTIVITIES IN CORDOBA

AQUASIERRA WATER PARK

Nestled just outside Córdoba, Aquasierra is a water paradise. With its vast array of exhilarating water slides, relaxing wave pools, and a serene lazy river, it promises endless fun. The park thoughtfully includes dedicated play zones for toddlers and younger children, ensuring a delightful day for the entire family. Surrounded by lush greenery, it's the perfect spot to cool off and create lasting memories.
Location: Carretera Córdoba, CO-3103, Km. 2, 5, 14420 Villafranca de Córdoba, Córdoba, Spain
Tip: Don't miss the "Black Hole" slide for a thrilling experience!
Website: www.aquasierra.es

CÓRDOBA HORSE SHOW AT CABALLERIZAS REALES

Experience the magic of Andalusian horses at the Royal Stables of Córdoba. The equestrian show, known as "Passion and Spirit of the Andalusian Horse," is a mesmerizing display of horsemanship that will captivate both children and adults.

Location: C. Caballerizas Reales, 1, 14004 Córdoba, Spain
Tip: It's recommended to book tickets in advance, especially during peak tourist seasons.
Website: www.cordobaecuestre.com/en/

CÓRDOBA CHILDREN'S CITY (CIUDAD DE LOS NIÑOS)

Nestled in the heart of Córdoba, the Ciudad de los Niños is more than just a playground. Spanning a vast area, this haven for children up to 12 years old offers a diverse range of play zones. From interactive water features to imaginative slides, climbing structures, and sandpits, every corner is designed to spark joy and creativity. Amidst the bustling city, it stands as a tranquil oasis where families can bond, children can explore freely, and laughter resonates.
Location: Av. Menéndez Pidal, s/n, 14004 Córdoba, Spain
Tip: It's advisable to bring a change of clothes for the kids, especially if they indulge in the water play areas.
Website: https://ciudaddelosninos.cordoba.es/

ILLUMINATED MONUMENTS AND EVENING STROLLS

MOSQUE-CATHEDRAL OF CÓRDOBA

As the sun sets, the Mezquita-Catedral takes on a mesmerizing glow, with its intricate arches and towering minaret illuminated against the night sky. The ambiance is further enhanced by the soft sounds of the evening prayers, making it a magical experience.

Location: Calle Cardenal Herrero, 1, Córdoba.

Tip: Consider joining a guided night tour to learn about the history and architecture of this iconic monument under the moonlight.

Website: www.mezquita-catedraldecordoba.es/en/

ROMAN BRIDGE

The Roman Bridge, spanning the Guadalquivir River, is a testament to Córdoba's rich history. At night, the bridge is beautifully lit, reflecting shimmering lights onto the water below. It's a popular spot for evening strolls, offering panoramic views of the city.

Location: Av. del Alcázar, s/n, Córdoba.

Tip: The bridge is pedestrian-friendly, making it perfect for a leisurely walk.

Website: www.turismodecordoba.org/puente-romano

ALCÁZAR DE LOS REYES CRISTIANOS

This fortress-palace, is a sight to behold when illuminated at night. The water features in the gardens add to the serene atmosphere, making it a romantic spot for couples.

Location: C. Caballerizas Reales, s/n, 14004 Córdoba, Spain

Tip: The Alcázar often hosts evening cultural events, from flamenco shows to classical concerts. Check their schedule for any special events during your visit.

Website: www.turismodecordoba.org/castle-of-the-christian-monarchs

BARS AND PUBS

SOCIEDAD PLATEROS

Located in a historic building, Taberna Sociedad Plateros offers a traditional Andalusian experience. With its rustic decor, wooden barrels, and vintage photographs, the ambiance is reminiscent of old-world Spain. The tavern is known for its extensive wine list and delicious tapas.

Location: C. María Auxiliadora, 25, 14002 Córdoba, Spain

Tip: Don't miss out on trying their signature Montilla-Moriles wines, which are a local favorite.

Website: www.sociedadplateros.co

BAR MORILES PATA NEGRA

A popular spot among locals and tourists alike, Bar Moriles Pata Negra offers a cozy setting with a wide range of Andalusian wines and tapas. The bar is especially known for its Iberian ham, which is a must-try.

Location: C. Antonio Maura, 23, 14004 Córdoba, Spain

Tip: Pair your wine with their assortment of cheeses for a delightful culinary experience.

Website: www.morilespatanegra.com/en/home/

LA BICICLETA

La Bicicleta is a trendy bar with a modern twist. The decor is inspired by bicycles, giving it a unique and quirky vibe. They offer a variety of craft beers, cocktails, and gourmet tapas. The bar also hosts live music events, making it a lively spot for night owls.

Location: C. Cardenal Gonzalez, 1, 14003 Córdoba, Spain

Tip: If you're a fan of craft beers, this is the place to be. Their beer menu is extensive and features local brews as well as international favorites.

Website: www.facebook.com/labicicletacordoba

NIGHTCLUBS AND DANCE CLUBS

LONG ROCK

If you're a rock music enthusiast, Long Rock Córdoba is the place to be. This lively club celebrates rock 'n' roll in all its forms, from classic rock anthems to modern hits. The decor is filled with rock memorabilia, and the club often hosts live bands and themed nights.

Location: Calle Teniente Braulio Laportilla, 6, 14008 Córdoba, Spain

Tip: Don't miss their signature cocktails, especially the ones named after rock legends.

Website: www.longrock.es/cordoba

BAMBÚ LOUNGE CLUB

A popular nightlife spot in Córdoba, Bambú Lounge Club boasts a vibrant atmosphere, great music, and a diverse crowd. Dance the night away and enjoy a cocktail in this centrally located club.

Location: Calle Conde de Robledo, 1, 14008 Córdoba, Spain

Tip: Check their social media for special events and promotions.

Website: www.facebook.com/BambuExperience

GOLDEN CLUB

Located in the heart of Córdoba, Golden Club stands out as a premier nightlife destination. This trendy dance club seamlessly blends modern beats with classic tunes, ensuring a musical experience for all. Its stylish interiors, combined with an always energetic crowd, create an electrifying atmosphere. Whether you're looking to dance or simply enjoy the ambiance, Golden Club promises an unforgettable evening.

Location: Historiador Diaz del Moral, 3 14008 Córdoba, Spain

Tip: Arrive early on weekends to avoid long lines and secure a good spot.

Website: www.facebook.com/goldenclubmusic/

LATE-NIGHT DINING

TABERNA RAFAÉ

Taberna Rafaé is a traditional Andalusian tavern that offers a cozy ambiance and delicious local dishes. Known for its authentic Cordoban cuisine, this establishment is a favorite among locals and tourists alike. Whether you're craving savory tapas or a hearty main dish, Taberna Rafaé has got you covered.

Location: Calle Deanes, 2, 14003 Córdoba, Spain

Tip: Don't leave without trying their signature "flamenquín" – a local delicacy made of ham and pork loin, breaded and fried to perfection.

Website: www.tabernarafae.com

SAN MIGUEL CASA EL PISTO

Fondly known as "Casa El Pisto", Taberna San Miguel is a historic tavern that has been serving Cordoban specialties for generations. The rustic interiors, adorned with vintage photographs and memorabilia, transport diners back in time. The menu boasts a variety of tapas, from classic "salmorejo" to succulent grilled meats.

Location: Plaza de San Miguel, 1, Córdoba.

Tip: The "berenjenas con miel" (fried eggplant with honey) is a must-try dish that perfectly balances sweet and savory flavors.

Website: www.casaelpisto.com

MEZQUITA CÉSPEDES

Located in the heart of Córdoba's historic center, Bodegas Mezquita Céspedes offers a unique dining experience. The establishment combines the charm of a traditional bodega with contemporary culinary delights. The extensive wine list features selections from Spain's finest vineyards, making it a paradise for wine enthusiasts.

Location: Calle Céspedes, 12, Córdoba.

Tip: Pair your meal with a glass of local "Montilla-Moriles" wine for an authentic Cordoban dining experience.

Website: www.bodegasmezquita.com/cespedes/

NIGHTLIFE AREAS

PLAZA DE LA CORREDERA

Plaza de la Corredera is one of Córdoba's most iconic squares. With its vast rectangular shape and historic architecture, it's a hub of activity both day and night. As the sun sets, the plaza comes alive with locals and tourists flocking to its many bars, cafes, and restaurants. The vibrant atmosphere, combined with live music and street performers, makes it a top spot for nightlife.

Location: Plaza de la Corredera, Córdoba.

Tip: Grab a seat at one of the terrace cafes, order a refreshing "tinto de verano" (summer wine), and soak in the lively ambiance.

Website: www.cordoba.es

CALLEJA DE LAS FLORES

Nestled in the heart of Córdoba's historic center, Calleja de las Flores is a picturesque alleyway adorned with blooming flowers and whitewashed walls. While it's a popular daytime attraction, the alley transforms into a romantic spot at night. Intimate bars and cafes line the street, offering a cozy setting for a nightcap or a leisurely chat.

Location: Calleja de las Flores, Córdoba.

Tip: The alley is particularly enchanting during the evening when the flowers are illuminated, creating a magical atmosphere. It's the perfect spot for a romantic evening stroll.

Website: www.turismodecordoba.org/calleja-de-las-flores-alley-of-the-flowers

PLAZA DEL POTRO

Plaza del Potro is a charming square named after the historic fountain featuring a prancing horse. Surrounded by Renaissance buildings and traditional Andalusian architecture, the plaza is a favorite gathering spot for locals. At night, the area buzzes with activity as people gather at the surrounding bars and tapas joints, making it a lively spot for nightlife.

Location: Plaza del Potro, Córdoba.

Tip: Visit the nearby "Posada del Potro", a historic inn turned cultural center, for a dose of Córdoba's rich history and culture.

Website: www.turismodecordoba.org/plaza-del-potro2

CORDOBA BY NIGHT

SAFETY TIPS

- Be aware of your surroundings and keep an eye on your belongings, as pickpocketing can be an issue in crowded areas.
- Stick to well-lit streets and avoid wandering into unfamiliar, poorly lit areas late at night.
- Use reputable taxi services or ride-sharing apps to get around at night, especially if you are unfamiliar with the area. **Tip:** Save the phone number of a trusted taxi company in your phone for convenience.
- When enjoying the vibrant nightlife, always keep your drink in sight and never accept drinks from strangers. **Tip:** Drinking responsibly and staying hydrated will help ensure a safer and more enjoyable night out.
- Keep emergency contact numbers handy, including local police and your country's embassy.
- Carry a photocopy of your passport and other important documents, leaving the originals in a safe place.

By following these tips and exploring the city by night, you'll be able to experience the magic and charm of the city while staying safe and having an unforgettable time.

ART, HISTORY AND ARCHITECTURE

Córdoba, gracefully poised in the sunlit realms of southern Spain's Andalusia, is a city where time seems to have left its most beautiful imprints. This ancient city, with its intertwining alleys and whitewashed walls, has been a crucible of cultures, each leaving behind a legacy of unparalleled art, profound history, and awe-inspiring architecture.

At the heart of Córdoba's artistic grandeur is the Mezquita, a monumental mosque-cathedral. Its forest of columns, adorned with red and white arches, is a testament to Islamic artistry, while the later Christian additions showcase the city's evolving religious tapestry. This architectural marvel stands as a symbol of Córdoba's harmonious blend of Moorish and Christian influences.

Yet, the Mezquita is but one chapter in Córdoba's artistic anthology. The Alcázar de los Reyes Cristianos, with its resplendent gardens and mosaics, echoes tales of monarchs and conquests. The city's Jewish Quarter, with its narrow lanes and Sephardic history, is a canvas of stories, art, and traditions that have transcended time.

Historically, Córdoba's significance peaked during its time as the capital of the Caliphate of Córdoba. This era saw the city evolve into a beacon of learning, culture, and architectural innovation, rivaling the grandeur of the world's most illustrious cities. Philosophers, poets, and scholars flocked to its libraries, making it a hub of enlightenment.

Architecturally, Córdoba is a symphony of styles. From Roman bridges and Islamic palaces to Renaissance plazas and Baroque chapels, the city is a living museum, each corner narrating a tale of its diverse past. The Roman Temple, a relic from ancient times, stands as a testament to Córdoba's Roman roots, while the Palacio de Viana, with its twelve courtyards, showcases the city's love for gardens and open spaces.

In essence, Córdoba is not just a destination; it's a journey. A journey through epochs, art forms, and architectural wonders. For the discerning traveler, Córdoba offers a timeless exploration of art, history, and architectural genius, capturing the soul of Andalusia in every stone and story.

ART AND CULTURE IN CORDOBA

MUSEO ARQUEOLÓGICO DE CÓRDOBA

The Archaeological Museum of Córdoba offers a deep dive into the city's rich history, spanning from prehistoric times to the Middle Ages. Housed in a Renaissance palace, the museum showcases a vast collection of artifacts, including Roman mosaics, Iberian sculptures, and Moorish relics. The museum's courtyard, with its beautiful arches and columns, is a testament to Córdoba's architectural splendor.

Location: Plaza de Jerónimo Páez, 7, Córdoba.
Tip: Don't miss the impressive Roman sculpture collection and the Moorish-era courtyard.
Website: www.turismodecordoba.org/archaeological-museum

MUSEO DE BELLAS ARTES

Córdoba's Fine Arts Museum, located in the former Hospital de la Caridad, showcases a remarkable collection of Spanish art from the Middle Ages to the 20th century. The museum's galleries are adorned with works by renowned artists such as Zurbarán, Valdés Leal, and local painter Antonio del Castillo. The serene atmosphere and stunning artworks make it a must-visit for art enthusiasts.

Location: Plaza del Potro 1, Córdoba.
Tip: Take your time exploring the museum's collection of Baroque paintings, which offer a glimpse into Spain's artistic golden age.
Website: www.turismodecordoba.org/fine-arts-museum

ART AND CULTURE IN CORDOBA

MUSEO JULIO ROMERO DE TORRES

Dedicated to Córdoba's most famous painter, Julio Romero de Torres, this museum celebrates the artist's unique style and passion for Andalusian culture. Housed in the same building as the Fine Arts Museum, the collection includes some of Romero de Torres' most iconic works, capturing the essence of Córdoba's traditions, landscapes, and people.
Location: Pl. del Potro, 1-4, 14002 Córdoba, Spain
Tip: The painting "La Chiquita Piconera," depicting a young coal girl, is one of the museum's highlights and a testament to the artist's mastery.
Website: https://museojulioromero.cordoba.es/

MUSEO TAURINO

The Bullfighting Museum of Córdoba delves into the world of Spanish bullfighting, a tradition deeply rooted in Andalusian culture. The museum traces the history of this controversial yet iconic sport, showcasing a collection of costumes, photographs, and memorabilia. Visitors can learn about the legendary matadors of Córdoba and the evolution of bullfighting techniques over the centuries.
Location: Pl. Maimónides, 3, 14004 Córdoba, Spain
Tip: The museum offers a balanced perspective on bullfighting, highlighting both its cultural significance and the ethical debates surrounding it.
Website: http://www.museotaurinodecordoba.es/

ART AND CULTURE IN CORDOBA

CASA DE SEFARAD

Located in the heart of Córdoba's Jewish Quarter, Casa de Sefarad is a tribute to the city's Sephardic Jewish heritage. The museum offers a glimpse into the life, culture, and contributions of the Jewish community in medieval Spain. Exhibits include artifacts, manuscripts, and interactive displays that tell the story of Jewish life in Córdoba before the expulsion in 1492.

Location: C. Judíos, 14004 Córdoba, Spain
Tip: Don't miss the section dedicated to famous Jewish scholars of Córdoba, such as Maimonides, whose teachings continue to influence Jewish thought worldwide.
Website: http://museocasadesefarad.com/

CENTRO DE FLAMENCO FOSFORITO

The Centro de Flamenco Fosforito is a cultural center dedicated to the art of flamenco. Located in the Posada del Potro, a historic inn mentioned in Cervantes' "Don Quixote," the center celebrates Córdoba's rich flamenco heritage. It offers exhibitions, workshops, and live performances, providing visitors with a deep dive into the world of flamenco music, dance, and culture. Named after Antonio Fernández Díaz "Fosforito," a renowned flamenco singer from Córdoba, the center is a testament to the city's vibrant artistic spirit.

Location: Pl. del Potro, 10, 14003 Córdoba, Spain
Tip: Attend one of the live flamenco shows to experience the passion and artistry of this traditional Andalusian art form.
Website: www.centroflamencofosforito.cordoba.es

HISTORICAL AND ARCHITECTURAL LANDMARKS IN CORDOBA

PALACIO DE LA MERCED

Once a convent founded in the 13th century, the Palacio de la Merced has undergone various transformations over the centuries. Today, it stands as the Provincial Government building. Its Baroque-style architecture is a marvel, showcasing a stunning façade, intricate detailing, and a grand cloister. The palace's history is palpable in every corner, from its majestic archways to its ornate ceilings. The courtyard, a harmonious blend of architecture and nature, is adorned with fountains and lush greenery, offering visitors a serene escape amidst the historical ambiance. This landmark is a testament to the artistic and architectural prowess of the period, reflecting Córdoba's rich heritage.
Location: Pl. de Colón, 15, 14001 Córdoba, Spain
Tip: The palace occasionally hosts cultural events and exhibitions, so it's worth checking the local listings during your visit.
Website: www.turismodecordoba.org/palace-of-la-merced

ALMÓDOVAR CASTLE

Almódovar Castle is a historical fortress in Córdoba, offering panoramic views of the surrounding landscapes. Notably used as a filming location for HBO's "Game of Thrones," the castle boasts a rich history and stunning architecture. Visitors can explore the various towers and learn about the civilizations that once occupied this landmark. A must-visit for history buffs and TV series enthusiasts.
Location: C. Castillo, 14720 Almodóvar del Río, Córdoba, Spain
Tip: Fans of "Game of Thrones" will recognize several filming locations within the castle. Consider taking a guided tour for a deeper dive into its history.
Website: www.castillodealmodovar.com

HISTORICAL AND ARCHITECTURAL LANDMARKS IN CORDOBA

PUERTA DE ALMODÓVAR

The Puerta de Almodóvar is one of the ancient gates of the medieval city of Córdoba. Located in the western part of the city, this gate served as a primary entrance during the Moorish era. It stands as a testament to the city's rich history, with its robust stone structure and archway. The surrounding area, with its cobblestone streets and whitewashed buildings, offers a glimpse into Córdoba's past. Nearby, you can also find the statue of the famous philosopher Seneca, who was born in Córdoba.
Location: Calle Cairuán, 14001 Córdoba, Spain.
Tip: Take a leisurely walk around the gate to explore the neighboring Judería (Jewish Quarter) and its many historical sites.
Website: www.turismodecordoba.org/the-almodovar-gate

CHAPEL OF SAN BARTOLOMÉ (CAPILLA DE SAN BARTOLOMÉ)

Nestled in the heart of the Jewish Quarter, the Chapel of San Bartolomé is a hidden gem that showcases the Mudejar architectural style of Córdoba. Built in the 15th century, this chapel boasts intricate plasterwork, wooden ceilings, and stunning tile mosaics. The combination of Christian and Islamic design elements reflects the city's rich cultural tapestry. The chapel's small size adds to its intimate and serene atmosphere, making it a peaceful retreat from the city's busier attractions.
Location: Calle Averroes, 14004 Córdoba, Spain.
Tip: The chapel is often overlooked by tourists, making it a perfect spot for those seeking a quiet and authentic experience of Córdoba's historical architecture.
Website: www.turismodecordoba.org/chapel-of-san-bartolome2

ARCHITECTURAL LANDMARKS IN CORDOBA

PALACIO DE VIANA (VIANA PALACE)

A true representation of Cordoban living from the 15th to 20th centuries, Palacio de Viana is often referred to as the "Patio Museum". With 12 different patios, each reflecting a unique period and style, visitors are taken on a journey through time. The palace itself houses an impressive collection of tapestries, furniture, and artwork, offering a glimpse into the aristocratic life of bygone eras.
Location: Pl. de Don Gome, 2, 14001 Córdoba, Spain.
Tip: Opt for a guided tour to get a deeper understanding of the history and significance of each patio and the artifacts within the palace.
Website: www.palaciodeviana.com

TORRE DE LA MALMUERTA (MALMUERTA TOWER)

An iconic octagonal tower built in the late 15th century, Torre de la Malmuerta stands as a sentinel of Córdoba's storied past. As an integral part of the ancient city walls, it was strategically erected on the remnants of a former gate from the Moorish era. The tower's intriguing name is steeped in local lore: it's said that a nobleman, consumed by jealousy, imprisoned and starved his wife within these very walls, accusing her of infidelity. While the veracity of this tale remains debated, the tower's allure is undeniable. Its vantage point offers sweeping panoramic views of Córdoba's architectural tapestry, juxtaposing the old with the new. This blend of history, legend, and scenic beauty makes the tower a must-visit attraction, drawing both history enthusiasts and those seeking the perfect cityscape view.
Location: 14001 Córdoba, Spain
Tip: Climb to the top for a breathtaking view of Córdoba's skyline, especially during sunset.
Website: www.turismodecordoba.org/the-malmuerta-tower

DAY TRIPS FROM CORDOBA

SIERRA DE HORNACHUELOS PARK
A sprawling natural reserve known for its diverse flora and fauna. The park is a haven for birdwatchers, with species like the imperial eagle and black vulture calling it home.
Location: Sierra de Hornachuelos, Córdoba, Spain. Distance: About 50 km from Córdoba.
Tip: Embark on one of the many hiking trails to explore the park's scenic beauty and spot its diverse wildlife.

ZUHEROS
A picturesque village nestled amidst the Sierras Subbéticas mountains, known for its Moorish castle and the Cueva de los Murciélagos (Bat Cave).
Location: Zuheros, Córdoba, Spain. Distance: About 70 km from Córdoba.
Tip: Visit the local cheese factories to sample the region's renowned sheep's cheese.

ALMODÓVAR DEL RÍO
A majestic fortress overlooking the Guadalquivir River, with roots dating back to Roman times. The castle offers panoramic views of the surrounding countryside.
Location: Almodóvar del Río, Córdoba, Spain. Distance: About 25 km from Córdoba.
Tip: Join a guided tour to delve into the castle's rich history and architectural marvels.

MONTILLA
The heart of Andalusia's wine country, Montilla is renowned for its vineyards and the production of Montilla-Moriles wines.
Location: Montilla, Córdoba, Spain. Distance: About 50 km from Córdoba.
Tip: Embark on a wine tasting tour to savor the region's signature Pedro Ximénez wine.

PRIEGO DE CÓRDOBA
A Baroque gem, this town boasts stunning churches, a Moorish castle, and the Fuente del Rey fountain.
Location: Priego de Córdoba, Córdoba, Spain. Distance: About 100 km from Córdoba.
Tip: Wander through the town's historic Jewish quarter, La Villa, to discover its charming alleys and squares.

DAY TRIPS FROM CORDOBA

LUCENA
Known as the "Pearl of the Sepharad", Lucena boasts a rich Jewish heritage, with landmarks like the Castle of Lucena and the Archaeological and Ethnological Museum.
Location: Lucena, Córdoba, Spain. Distance: About 60 km from Córdoba.
Tip: Visit the Church of San Mateo, a stunning example of Andalusian Gothic architecture.

RUTE
Famous for its aniseed liqueur and traditional Spanish sweets, Rute is a treat for the senses, especially during the Christmas season.
Location: Rute, Córdoba, Spain. Distance: About 110 km from Córdoba.
Tip: Explore the town's numerous museums dedicated to sweets, chocolate, and anise.

CABRA
Nestled at the foot of the Subbética mountains, Cabra is known for its thermal baths, historic churches, and the Villa Romana de los Remedios.
Location: Cabra, Córdoba, Spain. Distance: About 80 km from Córdoba.
Tip: Relax in the Balneario Aguas de Cabra, a spa with therapeutic waters.

MONTORO
A picturesque town on the banks of the Guadalquivir River, Montoro is known for its olive oil production and the Montoro-Adamuz Natural Park.
Location: Montoro, Córdoba, Spain. Distance: About 45 km from Córdoba.
Tip: Visit the San Bartolomé church, a blend of Gothic and Renaissance styles.

BAENA
A town with a rich history, Baena is home to the Iberian-Roman archaeological site of Torreparedones and is renowned for its olive oil.
Location: Baena, Córdoba, Spain. Distance: About 60 km from Córdoba.
Tip: Explore the Baena Archaeological Museum to delve into the town's ancient past.

END NOTE

Córdoba, where ancient history intertwines with vibrant modernity, presents a mesmerizing tapestry of cultures and eras. From the awe-inspiring Mezquita-Catedral to the lively plazas of the Jewish Quarter, every alley and archway in this Andalusian gem whispers tales of its illustrious past. As you wander through its cobblestone streets, indulge in traditional Andalusian fare, and soak in its rich mosaic of Moorish, Christian, and Jewish influences, you'll discover the soul of Córdoba. Whether you're captivated by its architectural wonders, historical narratives, or culinary adventures, Córdoba promises an expedition filled with enduring memories.

Dive deep into the heart of this Andalusian treasure!

Unlock a world of unforgettable experiences with Tailored Travel Guides! As your go-to source for personalized and meticulously crafted travel guides, we ensure that every adventure is uniquely yours. Our team of dedicated travel experts and local insiders design each guide with your preferences, interests, and travel style in mind, providing you with the ultimate customized travel experience. Embark on your next journey with confidence, knowing that Tailored Travel Guides has got you covered. To explore more exceptional destinations and discover a treasure trove of additional guides, visit www.tailoredtravelguides.com. or our collection available

on **Amazon** at this link: www.amazon.com/stores/Tailored-Travel-Guides/author/B0C4TV5TZX or

on **Google Play**, at this link: https://play.google.com/store/books/author?id=Tailored+Travel+Guides

on **Etsy**, at this link: https://tailoredtravelguides.etsy.com

Happy travels, and here's to a lifetime of remarkable memories!

Join our Tailored Travel Guides Network for more benefits by accessing this link:
https://mailchi.mp/d151cba349e8/ttgnetwork
Or by scanning the QR code

Loved Your Journey With Our Guide? ⭐
Your feedback makes a world of difference! If our guide helped you explore or enjoy your destination, we would be thrilled if you could take a moment to leave us a 5-star review on our product page.🙏

Simply click the link or go to any of our product pages on your preferred retailer website and **share your recommendations.**

https://www.amazon.com/stores/Tailored-Travel-Guides/author/B0C4TV5TZX

Thank you for chosing Tailored Travel Guides!

Discover your journey!

ALSO IN THE SEARIES SERIES

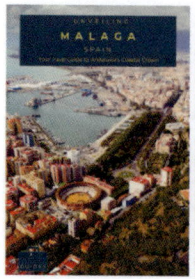 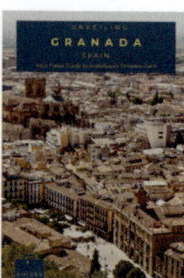   

CHECK OUT THE ITALY UNCOVERED SERIES

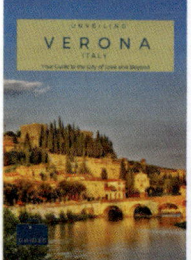   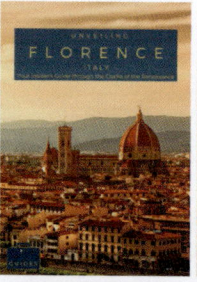 

 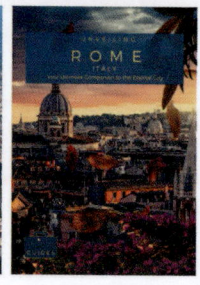  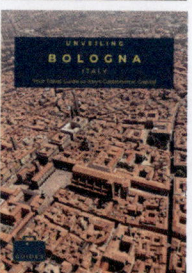 

CHECK OUT THE FRANCE UNVEILED SERIES

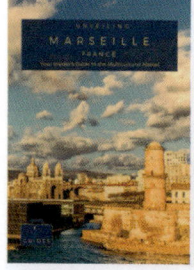 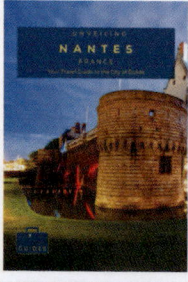   

 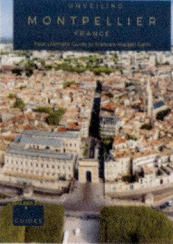   

Printed in Dunstable, United Kingdom